Cursive Writing with Ms. Penn

Book 1

by
Annie Lena Day

Cover design by
Angela Oltmann

Comics by
Awesomesatyr.com

Graphics by
Shaily &
Helen Graphics

Dedicated to my own little Scribbles Kids

~ Owen & Eva ~

Copyright 2019
ISBN 978-0-9600277-4-3

The material in this book is intended for individual use only.
No part of this publication may be transmitted, reproduced, stored,
or recorded in any form without written permission from the author.

This book is different from other cursive workbooks. It does not start with the letter A and work through the alphabet to Z. It starts with the letters that are the simplest to form and gradually increases in difficulty. It teaches cursive the way I taught in my classroom … in a light hearted and sequential manner with lots of humor and a bit of silliness.

You and your student will share a few laughs as you work through this book. You'll meet cartoon characters who explain the fine points of writing for each lesson. Ms. Penn, the teacher, writes on the board to explain letter formation. The Scribbles, who are the students, show off their work and add a few of their own comments. They also show some of the common mistakes that new writers make.

There are animals in the class too and they all speak up! The class pet is a fish. (Some mice and a worm also live in the room.)

To accompany this book, there are plenty of resources available online. If you are ever unsure how to form a letter, look on YouTube at "Cursive Writing with Ms. Penn." There you'll find demonstrations for many lessons and some bonus lessons too.

Some pages in this book teach how to change print writing to cursive writing. This is a slightly more difficult skill than just tracing and copying words. The answer key for those pages is available on my website www.AnnieLenaDay.com. Just click on the link that says, "Answer Key for Cursive Book 1."

And for those who want more guided practice ... there are extra pages at www.AnnieLenaDay.com These pages are labeled with lesson numbers. You can use them for extra practice after the appropriate lesson has been completed.

There are many different ways to write in cursive and I have chosen to teach the simplest way to form each letter. Much practice is required to master cursive, and this book is a starting point. It covers only the lower-case letters. The capital letters are taught in book 2.

I hope this book will bring much joy and pride to your child. I also hope that it will be treasured! When completed, tuck it away as a keepsake of your student's childhood! You'll appreciate the memories in years to come.

Annie Lena Day

Lower-case "L"

Practice two L's together. Leave a space.

Lower-case "e"

Leave a space between your words.

See lesson 1 on YouTube at *"Cursive Writing with Ms. Penn"*

Lower-case "t"

Lower-case "i"

See lesson 2 on YouTube at ***"Cursive Writing with Ms. Penn"***.

Lower-case "u"

Lower-case "w"

we

wet

well

will

bill

See lesson 3 on YouTube at *"Cursive Writing with Ms. Penn"*.

Lower-case "n"

n n
nn

Lower-case "m"

m m
mm
tim

ten

melt

See lesson 4 on YouTube at *"Cursive Writing with Ms. Penn"*.
Find extra practice at *www.AnnieLenaDay.com*

Lower-case "j"

j j

Lower-case "y"

y y

jet

yet

my

See lesson 5 on YouTube at *"Cursive Writing with Ms. Penn"*.

Lower-case "c"

c c

Lower-case "a"

a a

at

at

call

mice

See lesson 6 on YouTube at *"Cursive Writing with Ms. Penn"*. Also see **Bonus #1**
Find extra practice at *www.AnnieLenaDay.com*

Practice What You've Learned

mat

mate

mine

mine

met

More Practice

meet

mame

came

mail

mail

Lesson 8

Lower-case "d"

Lower-case "g"

See lesson 9 on YouTube at *"Cursive Writing with Ms. Penn"*.
Find extra practice at *www.AnnieLenaDay.com*

Write these words in cursive.

cut

cute

tag

tug

What do scissors do?

Lesson 10
Find the answer key at www.AnnieLenaDay.com
Also see Bonus #1 on Youtube.

Write these words in cursive.

line

lime

mile

cat

What animal is this?

Lesson 11
Find the answer key at **www.AnnieLenaDay.com**

See how to make this letter on YouTube at "Cursive Writing with Ms. Penn"

Lower-case "o"

o o

double "o"

oo

to

too

moon

See lesson 12 on YouTube at **"Cursive Writing with Ms. Penn"**.
Find extra practice is at www.AnnieLenaDay.com

Write these words in cursive.

tool

toe

late

date

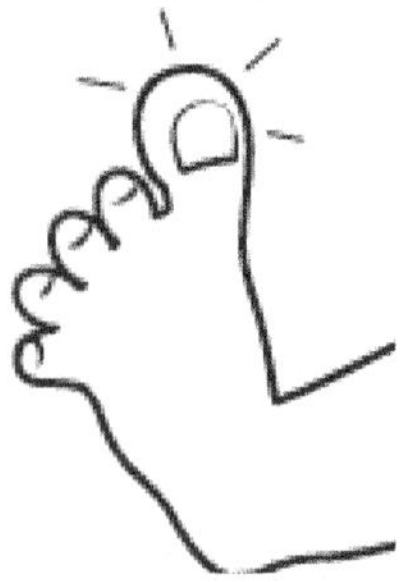

Which word is this?

Write these words in cursive.

dog

day

way

away

What animal is this?

Lesson 14
Find the answer key at **www.AnnieLenaDay.com**

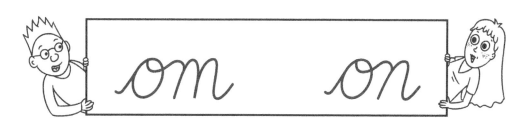

om

om

done

done

ome

wom

Write the word for the picture.

Practice What You've Learned

mill

wilt

mot

men

man

More Practice

went

wing

come

cone

coat

Lesson 17

Lower-case "v"

Lower-case "x"

Lower-case "z"

See lesson 18 on YouTube at **"Cursive Writing with Ms. Penn"**.
Find extra practice is at www.AnnieLenaDay.com

Lower-case "p"

p p

pp

Lower-case "q"

q q

qu

quiz

quill

puzzle

See lesson 19 on YouTube at *"Cursive Writing with Ms. Penn"*.
Also see **Bonus #2**

Write these words in cursive.

apple

have

been

pill

Which word goes with this picture?

Lesson 20
Find the answer key at **www.AnnieLenaDay.com**

Write these words in cursive.

wait

tax

pig

zoom

Which word goes with this picture?

Lesson 21
Find the answer key at **www.AnnieLenaDay.com**

Lower-case "h"

h h

Lower-case "k"

k k

hid

hide

kid

kind

See lesson 22 on YouTube at ***"Cursive Writing with Ms. Penn"***.

Lower-case "b"

b b

bb

Lower-case "f"

f f

ff

bull

fluff

fluffy

See lesson 23 on YouTube at **"Cursive Writing with Ms. Penn"**.
Find extra practice is at www.AnnieLenaDay.com

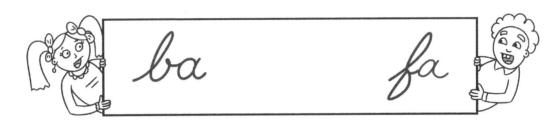

bat

fat

ball

fall

falling

boy

boat

bowl

foot

fool

Write these words in cursive.

dug

dig

jug

flame

Which word goes with this picture?

Lesson 26

Write these words in cursive.

dad

daddy

juggle

jiggle

Which word is this?

Lesson 27
Find the answer key at **www.AnnieLenaDay.com**

Lower-case "r"

r r

rr

Lower-case "s"

s s

ss

sun

sun

rake

See lesson 28 on YouTube at **"Cursive Writing with Ms. Penn"**.
Find extra practice is at www.AnnieLenaDay.com

Write these words in cursive.

rat

sat

bee

see

Which word is this? Add "s" to a word.

Lesson 29
Find the answer key at **www.AnnieLenaDay.com.**
Also see Bonus #3 on YouTube.

Write these words in cursive.

soap

soup

bath

flat

Which word is this?

Lesson 30
Find the answer key at **www.AnnieLenaDay.com**.

wr

write

write

who

whom

Lesson 31

Write these words in cursive.

writer

wreck

when

where

Which word is this?

Lesson 32
Find the answer key at **www.AnnieLenaDay.com.**

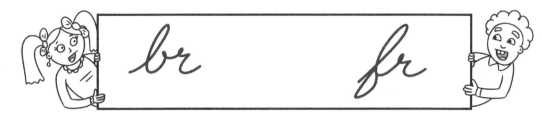

br

fr

broom

from

breeze

freeze

Write these words in cursive.

bring

brag

brain

brown

Which word goes with the picture?

Lesson 34
Find the answer key at **www.AnnieLenaDay.com.**

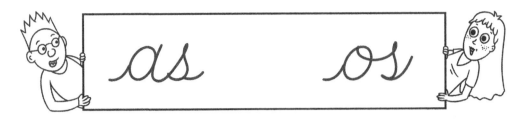

as

os

bas

boss

cat

cot

Write these words in cursive.

lass

last

lost

baseball

Which word goes with the picture?

Lesson 36
Find the answer key at **www.AnnieLenaDay.com.**

or

ar

born

born

more

Lesson 37

Write these words in cursive.

farm

door

stare

stair

Which word goes with the picture?

Lesson 38
Find the answer key at **www.AnnieLenaDay.com.**

wi

wit

win

wind

window

with

wild

Write these words in cursive.

whip

wizard

what

wife

Which word is this?

Lesson 40
Find the answer key at www.AnnieLenaDay.com.

vi

vi

vine

living

village

vision

waving

Write these words in cursive.

van

unicorns

fancy

zero

Take "s" off one of the words above.

Lesson 42

na

na

nose

nose

nature

nature

nourish

nourish

maximum

maximum

60 Lesson 43

Write these words in cursive.

zone

quart

witch

which

Which word is this?

Dear Parents and Teachers,

Thank you for buying this book. I hope you found it enjoyable and educational for your student. You can help others find this book by leaving a review.

Cursive writing is a skill and like all skills it takes practice to become proficient. Keep writing in cursive and with lots of practice your student will develop fluency.

Book 2 in this series teaches all the capital letters. Book 3 is subtitled, *Finding Your Style* and it shows the many different ways to write in cursive. It helps learners to appreciate the individuality we all have -- even with something as traditional as cursive writing.

Annie Lena Day

Keep smiling!

See you in Book 2!

Extra Writing Paper

Download and print more paper from www.AnnieLenaDay.com

Made in the USA
Coppell, TX
14 November 2019